WHY DIDN'T MY SPELL WORK?

How To Troubleshoot Any Magical Spell & Set Your Witchcraft Up For Success

JULIE WILDER

CONTENTS

Also by Julie Wilder   v

INTRODUCTION
1. Don't Forget Your Free Book!   3
2. My Failed Spell   5
3. My Magical Philosophy   11
4. How To Use This Book   15
5. How Do You Know Your Spell Failed?   19

EXTERNAL REASONS YOUR SPELL DIDN'T WORK
6. You Performed The Spell In The Wrong Location.   29
7. Your Magical Tools Were Holding Conflicting Energy.   37
8. Your Altar Wasn't Set Up Right.   43
9. You Wore The Wrong Clothes.   47
10. You Didn't Take Enough Action After Your Spell.   53
11. You Didn't Word Your Spell Correctly.   61
12. You Told Someone About Your Spell And They Reacted Negatively.   67
13. You Didn't Plan For Success.   71

INTERNAL REASONS YOUR SPELL DIDN'T WORK
14. You Didn't Ground Yourself First.   75
15. You Weren't Feeling Your Best On The Day You Cast Your Spell.   79
16. You Got Upset When Someone Else Got What You Desire.   83

17. You Didn't Ask For Enough (Or You Asked For Too Much). 87
18. Your Magical Intention Was Too Specific. 91
19. Your Magical Intention Was Not Specific Enough. 95
20. You Made Excuses For Why You Can't Manifest Your Spell. 99
21. You're Scared. 107
22. You Were Too Attached To The Outcome. 115
23. You Are Stuck In An Unhelpful Energetic Pattern. 121
24. You Didn't Wait Long Enough. 125
25. You Didn't Actually Want It. 127

FINAL THOUGHTS ON SPELLCASTING
26. My Favorite Spellcasting Hack 133
27. Why Witchcraft Is Like Driving A Car 137

Also by Julie Wilder 141

Also by Julie Wilder

What Type of Witch Are You?
How to Become A Witch
Why Didn't My Spell Work?
Beginner Witch's Guide to Grimoires
Tarot for Beginner Witches

INTRODUCTION

Don't Forget Your Free Book!

If you want to learn more ways to practice simple, secular witchcraft, be sure to pick up a **copy of this free book of spells**, and my **free Beginner Witch Starter kit** with printables, correspondences, meditations, and magical journaling prompts. Use the link below to get both of those!

https://whitewitchacademy.com/freebies

My Failed Spell

Hi there! I'm Julie Wilder, and I'm a witch. I cast spells. Sometimes they work. Sometimes they totally blow up in my face.

Can you relate?

Let me tell you about one of the blowing-up-in-the-face spells.

I was in my early thirties, and I decided that one of my ex-boyfriends who I dated ten years ago was cosmically linked to me, and that we were DESTINED to be together.

Sound stalkery yet?

Oh, just you wait. There's more.

For the sake of not getting sued, let's call this man "Lou"—short for Lucifer. (Ha—I kid, I kid!)

But let's roll with that name.

So Lou and I met when we were in our early

twenties. We immediately hit it off, and had a short but passionate relationship. Eventually, he dumped me in a very mundane way. He ghosted me before ghosting was even a thing. Basically, he had to travel out of state for two months for work, and he stopped talking to me.

I never really got over him, and on some level, I suspect he never got over me.

Over the next ten years, I'd get messages from him every now and them. They were flirty and funny. We'd talk for a few days online before he would disappear again. Each time, I would cry to my therapist about it. A few months would pass, and I'd assume I'd never hear from him again. Then he'd send me another out-of-the-blue message, and it would break my heart all over again when he stopped responding.

As time went on, I became more spiritual. I "felt" like Lou was my spiritual true love, and decided to set about pursuing him through witchcraft. (And yes, I know it's frowned upon in the magical community to perform love spells for a specific person, but so what? I chose to do it anyway.)

During that time, I performed lots of love spells. I basically immersed myself in magic. As a result, I manifested a lot of amazing things—a car, money, and a big leap forward with my business.

I felt like I was in total alignment—that I could do ANYTHING.

I even felt like I was growing closer to Lou as well. We talked more online, sometimes having conversations late into the night. We shared private stuff, told each other how we felt, and talked about meeting up in person. Then I decided to move to his city—which, in my defense, wasn't that big of a deal. I was a digital nomad, so I moved all the time.

Things seemed to be going in the right direction for Lou and me, and I was excited. In my mind, being with Lou was a done deal. We'd meet up in his city, date, fall in love, and we'd end up getting married.

That was my plan anyway.

All the other areas of my life were going well, so I trusted my love spells to work, too.

You can imagine my surprise when, on the night I arrived in my new city, I discovered that Lou had just gotten *married*—to someone else.

It gave me a serious case of magical whiplash. I had to deal with the pain of a broken heart. On top of that, my blotched love spell shattered my faith in myself and in my magic. I started to question my ENTIRE witchcraft practice because the only possible two conclusions I could draw from my spell not working were:

1. I'm not the powerful witch I thought I was.
2. Magic isn't real.

Both of those possibilities were upsetting. It majorly shook my confidence to the point where I actually stopped believing in magic.

My friends would text me and ask me to draw cards for them, and I'd say, "No. That stuff isn't real and it's just going to mess with your head."

They'd ask me for tips for what spells to do for the full moon, and I'd say, "Don't waste your time."

They'd mention seeing "signs" or "synchronicities", and I'd say, "You're just seeing what you want to see."

It was a sad time for me. Magic was what made my life fun. It made every day feel like an adventure and that I was the brave heroine moving through life with courage and wonder.

Without magic, life was boring.

To cope with my grim new reality, I started writing what would be my first paranormal mystery novel. I basically didn't want anything to do with real magic, so I created my own magical world to "live" in.

That was one of the amazing things that came out of this whole disaster. I've now completed seven novels, and it makes me so happy to think about people enjoying my stories!

It took about twelve months to work through all of the heartache and to take back control of my life. Slowly, I started to believe in magic again. I found myself wanting to draw tarot cards. I'd smile when I came across something that felt like a sign from the universe. I even started performing small spells.

I had to make sense of why some spells worked and some didn't. For example, why had magic gotten me everything I wanted in life—except the guy I loved? Did I do something wrong? Did I get too attached to the outcome? Did I push too hard?

I began to dive deeper into witchcraft, reading books, talking to other witches, and doing my own experimentations. I have some theories on why my spell with Lou didn't work out, and I hope this book can help you make sense of your own magical outcomes.

My goal is to inspire you to approach your magic with curiosity, playfulness, and courage. And if you only take one thing from this book, let it be this: **the reason your spell didn't work is not because you aren't powerful.**

Never doubt your power, my witchy friend. That's one thing you can always be sure of.

My Magical Philosophy

My philosophy is different from other witches in some ways, so it may or may not be your jam. To help you decide if you're the type of witch who will benefit from this book, **I'm going to tell you why I believe most spells fail right here at the beginning!**

Energy.

That's it.

I personally believe that when spells don't work it's likely because the energy that was used to power the spell did not match the energy of the spell's intention.

If that didn't make sense to you, don't worry. I'll go into a more detailed explanation about how to shift your energy to match the energy of your intention in this book. Consider this your brief introduction to my magical philosophy.

I'll say it again, spells fail because of misaligned energy.

Sometimes the misaligned energy comes from the magical tools used. Sometimes it's the location you chose to cast the spell in. Sometimes the issue comes from the energy of the spellcaster themselves.

My methods of magic are sometimes viewed as controversial because I personally don't subscribe to the idea that certain magical tools can only be used for specific intentions. For example, some witches believe only certain crystals can be used for cleansing spaces. I disagree. I think it comes down to energy, and energy alone. If your magical tool is charged with energy that *matches your intention* (whether the tool is traditionally used for that intention or not), I believe that tool can be very powerful and effective in that particular spell.

In my opinion, if you deeply believe that your amethyst crystal can cleanse your magical space, it will do just that.

I also focus heavily on how to manipulate energy within yourself, and that's because I believe the energy of the spellcaster is one of the most powerful elements in your magic. You are full of energy, and that energy is going to help power your magic.

After reading this book, you'll understand how energy affects spells. You'll also know how to begin troubleshooting your own spells, so that you'll never have to wonder, "Why didn't my spell work?"

How To Use This Book

I set this book up to be a reference book for witches looking to troubleshoot their spells. The first part of the book is going to cover the most common reasons for spells not working. I've separated all the common reasons into two categories—reasons related to external factors and reasons related to internal factors.

The external factors section will address things like the location of your spell, what you are wearing when you cast the spell, and the energy of your magical tools. These are all things that are outside of you and your personal energy. The internal factors section will cover things like energetic blocks, mindset work, false beliefs, fears, and general resistance that can hinder your spellwork.

For this book, I've selected these reasons for why spells sometimes fail based on my years of studying and researching witchcraft, my own personal experiences, and conversations that I've had with other witches. Each reason will have its own section that will include a detailed explanation and suggestions on how to move though that particular obstacle. Then, you can try your spell again and see if you get a different outcome!

I chose this format because I want you to be able to look at the table of contents and skip to the sections that you feel are most relevant to troubleshooting your particular spell.

You can also use this book as an oracle by asking the universe to lead you to the reason your particular spell didn't work. Then open the book and read whatever page you land on. (If you're reading the ebook, pick a number and read the corresponding section.)

Remember, this is by no means a full list of all the possible factors that affect your spell because the world of magic is big and diverse. I couldn't possibly fit all the reasons into a book, and I'm sure there are some reasons that we haven't even thought of because of our limited human perspective.

As you're reading this book, I invite you to experiment with the different ways to shift your energy to see what works best for you. Despite what some witches will tell you, one size does not fit all in magic. You'll find that your personality is better suited to certain magical practices. Think of all the unique ways people choose to dress or what foods they enjoy. There is a huge variety in those preferences. The same goes with magic.

Which leads me to my next point.

If you're looking for a book that will tell you there is one way to cast an effective spell, you're not going to like this book.

As a writer and entrepreneur, I've spent years looking for "the secret formula" to productivity so that I can skip to the front of the line and get my prize!

I've bought courses and products that promise to help me write faster and better. I've talked to lots of writers to find out if it's best to write in the morning, the evening, at home, in a cafe, after a snack, on an empty stomach, etc.

What I've discovered is that there's no "best way" for every writer. The only way to figure out how you write best is to try many different processes and pay attention to how you feel and how productive you are. Keep doing the things that work for you and let go of the rest. It's as simple as that.

I believe witchcraft is just like writing. You will figure out what works best for you through your personal experiences.

For me, witchcraft is very much intuition-based. For most of my life, I didn't trust myself. I believed everyone else was smarter, wiser, more creative, and more experienced than I was. I looked to others for the answers, always asking questions and looking for feedback. My life began to shift considerably when I started looking for answers within. My confidence and happiness increased, along with my self-care practices, my financial situation, my relationships with loved ones, and my business!

That's what I want to share with you in all of the books I write. I want to give you magical methods that help you take back your power and grow in happiness and confidence.

You *do* have all the answers inside of you.

You won't find them in other people or in your tarot cards, and you definitely won't find them in this book.

The witchy answers you seek will likely come to you as you explore the processes discussed in this book in your own personal magical practice.

How Do You Know Your Spell Failed?

Well, this is obvious, isn't it? You know your spell didn't work because you're not snuggling in the arms of your ideal lover, sunbathing on the beaches of the French Riviera admiring your $500 swimsuit, or waking up in your beautiful mansion in the Colorado mountains.

You know your spell didn't work because you had set an intention prior to casting your spell, and that intention did not happen.

(An intention is basically a vision for what your spell's ideal outcome would be—it's how you want your life to change as a result of your spell.)

I personally believe that magic is always working. Sometimes it works in exactly the way you hoped it would. Sometimes it takes a weird, twisty road that you couldn't have imagined in your wildest dreams.

That's all part of the fun, right?

The overall concepts I build my witchcraft practice around are Law of Attraction and Sympathetic Magic. I'm going to explain them here, but if you want a more in-depth look at these concepts, check out my book, *"How To Become A Witch"* (www.whitewitchacademy.com/books).

Law of Attraction is the idea that everything has a vibration—literally everything. This includes people, animals, homes, situations, experiences, objects, money, success, opportunities, love, and more. You can think of a "vibration" as a specific frequency of energy. Law of Attraction states that similar vibrations naturally attract other similar vibrations. If you are vibrating at the frequency of $100,000, you will attract $100,000.

Law of Attraction is also why things like visualization meditations work so well. It's not just witches doing those meditations. It's CEOs, politicians, actors, and athletes, too. When you take some time to visualize your ideal life or something you want to get good at, you are basically immersing your mind, body and spirit in the "vibration" of whatever you're visualizing. Energetically speaking, you are shifting your current vibration to align with your ideal vibration. Law of Attraction is then able to close that energetic gap between where you are and where you want to be so you can get that thing you want.

Boom. Magic.

Sympathetic magic is the idea that objects, colors, or energies that you use on your altar or in your magic will draw ideas, situations, and anything with matching energies towards you as a result of a spell, ritual, or meditation that you perform.

For example, you'll see a lot of spells that use colors to represent different intentions such as green for money spells (the color of abundant nature or of paper money in the US) or blue for communication spells (the color of the throat chakra). This works in magic because you have decided that these colors represent what you desire (or your intention) and therefore, they are magnetized to attract your desire.

Got all that?

If not, keep on reading. I'll say that same thing a million more times throughout this book.

I'll also use the word *manifest* a lot in this book. In the context of magic, "manifesting" means to bring about an outcome. For example, you might hear a witch say, "I manifested $100 with a money spell."

Before we get into the reasons why a spell didn't work, I want to take a couple more pages to talk about the way I've seen spells manifest in my own life as a result of my witchcraft practice.

There are three main outcomes to any spell:

1. You got exactly what you wanted and you're totally psyched about it.

2. You didn't see any change from your spell.

3. You didn't get what you wanted and you're confused or discouraged.

If you experience the first outcome, give yourself a pat on the back. Yay for you, witch! Celebrate this moment. It doesn't always happen like that! (Also, if you celebrate when your spells work, your spells will be more likely to manifest in the future because of the way Law of Attraction works. Basically, if you're a witch who gives lots of attention to your successful spells, you will likely experience more successful spells.)

If you experience the second or third outcomes, I invite you to browse this book to get ideas for why things happened the way they did.

What I don't want you to do is beat yourself up, and I really, really don't want you to think FOR ONE SECOND that you're a "bad" witch.

You're not. You literally cannot be a bad witch because you are an energetic being, and because of that, you have a natural ability to manipulate energy.

Another thing to keep in mind when you think your spell didn't work is to understand that your spell probably did SOMETHING. You likely made *some* kind of magical impact on your reality even if

WHY DIDN'T MY SPELL WORK?

you don't see it or understand it. Maybe your spell is just taking a long time, or maybe it brought about an outcome you didn't intend. (We'll discuss that more in this book.)

But you probably created some sort of energetic change in your world—let that be an encouragement to you.

Personally, I've performed money spells for years before the money started to show up. I'd get little bursts of money here and there. I'd win raffles and get raises. But the lasting, meaningful, consistent flow of money was a very slow burn.

Now that I've built up a little momentum in my work, I can tell you that it was worth it. The stress, worry, and risk I dealt with while throwing spaghetti at the wall and following my dream to be a writer gave me the knowledge and wisdom I needed to thrive once success started to manifest in my life.

My long and winding road to money WAS part of my magic. I was forced to learn a lot of lessons along the way, and because of that I've acquired the knowledge to write witchcraft books (which make me money). The book you're reading right now is the universe's answer to my years of money spells.

Can spells work immediately? Yes.

Can quick spells create lasting success? Totally.

But for me, it was helpful to look at the results of the spells with a patient, optimistic curiosity.

I often remind myself that in the physical world

that we all inhabit right now, change usually happens slowly

If you want gym-perfect muscles, you've got to put on a workout video or get yourself to the local gym. You also might need to change your diet.

Even then, change is going to be slow. I read somewhere on the internet (so it's got to be true, right? LOL) that it takes three months to see significant changes in your body and that it takes one year to completely overhaul your body composition. In this physical realm, changing your body is not typically instant.

Can a spell give you gym-perfect muscles without nutrition changes and exercise?

I believe yes. In the book, *Talent is Overrated*, the author writes about a study that was done that showed actual physiological differences in people who visualized working out.

Whaaaaaaaatttttt?

Cool, right?

That's something that even stumps my most pragmatic friends.

There are still other ways to change your body. Maybe your wellness spell can manifest the money for a medical procedure that changes your body. Maybe you get prescribed some medication for a mental health disorder that gives you more energy to exercise. Maybe you marry a chef who only cooks healthy, nutrient-packed meals and you forget all about your sugar cravings. (Please understand that this is all hypothetical. I'm not a doctor or any kind of health care professional. I'm also not recommending or discouraging any of these processes. I'm just throwing out ideas so you can see the numerous, very abstract ways a spell can manifest.)

We live in a huge, fantastical world full of the inspired creations and discoveries of the smart, creative people who came before us. The universe can bring about your spells in all kinds of crazy ways.

I believe that everything that happens to me is connected. One thing leads to another leads to another.

That's magic right there.

EXTERNAL REASONS YOUR SPELL DIDN'T WORK

You Performed The Spell In The Wrong Location.

Y ou ever walk into a store or cafe and think, "OMG, I love this place. This is my kind of place!" That reaction is you picking up on the energy of a space.

Conversely, have you ever strolled into a room and felt uncomfortable energy? This can include feeling unwanted emotions or feeling "heavy" or "tired" for no reason. Sometimes witches will have thoughts or see mental images of things that reflect the energy of the space. Whatever the energy, it will likely have an effect (big or small) on everyone and everything in that space. That energy will also have a significant impact on your spell.

Maybe you've had that experience with different cities, different rooms of a house, or different spots out in nature.

Consider getting into the habit of noticing if different emotions come up when you are in certain areas. You might even want to write it down in your grimoire or journal. That can be useful information to you when you're deciding on where to cast a spell.

If you perform a spell in a space that holds energy that doesn't align with your magical intention, that could be the reason your spell took a long time to manifest, or maybe never manifested at all.

For example, if you performed a love spell while sitting on the bed you shared with an ex-lover, the energy of sadness, loss, and a messy breakup may be lingering in that space. That energy can have a negative impact on your spell. If you're performing a love spell, you're going to want to perform that spell in a location that makes you, personally, feel loved. It's great if you can pick somewhere that makes you feel romantically loved, but really, any kind of love will work for a love spell. If your mom is the only one who loves you, perform your love spell in the living room where you and your mom have spent some fun, quality time playing Scrabble.

Another example is with money spells. You want to make sure the location where you're performing that spell doesn't have any of that scarcity energy floating around. When I lived in a tiny apartment with a leaky roof, I chose to perform my abundance spells in the woods of the Blue Ridge mountains where everything felt lovely and abundant—the leaves on the trees, the air I breathed, and bright blue sky. From that location, I was able to cast powerful wealth and abundance spells that changed my mindset and my quality of life.

Some witches have a dedicated space in their home for spellcasting. They regularly cleanse the space or charge the space to make sure the energy is going to help, not hinder, whatever kind of magic they are performing on that particular day.

If you're like me, and you do not currently have a designated space for magic—or you just want a change of scenery—you can perform the spell in a place that already holds energy that matches your intention.

It's also important for you to feel comfortable in that location. It should be somewhere you know you won't be distracted or disturbed. It's hard to focus on spellcasting when you're worried about your roommate bursting into your room and judging you for sitting in a circle of tea lights and crystals. You also don't want it to be somewhere that you'll feel self-conscious while spellcasting.

For me, this means I probably won't be spellcasting in a crowded park or in my corner booth at Panera. I'd feel like everyone was watching me. They probably aren't because what do they care?

Still, I would FEEL as if their eyes were on me, and that could potentially dilute my focus on my magical intention. That's just me, though. If you can block out the whole world while you're spellcasting, then go for it. Just be sure that the location you choose is helping your spell, not hindering it!

How To Shift The Energy

You have two options here. You can shift the energy of a space to match your intention or you can choose a new location that already matches your ideal energy.

If you opt to shift the energy of the space, you'll want to do two things—cleanse the space and then charge the space.

There are many ways to cleanse your space.

Here are a few of my go-to methods.

There's the white light meditation that I wrote about in my free book (available at www.whitewitchacademy.com/freebies). It's where you sit in the middle of your space, close your eyes and visualize white light floating down from the sky and filling the room. (There are also a couple other cleansing methods discussed in that book, and again, it's totally free. You're welcome xoxo!)

Another way to cleanse your space is with moon water. To do this, fill a glass jar with water. Place the water outside or near a window overnight at the time of the new moon—a very cleansing phase of the lunar cycle! Then spritz the water throughout the space or pour it on a cloth and wipe down the floor of your space. You might also want to use it on the walls (if it's not going to mess up your wallpaper) and pay special attention to places where energy tends to gather (window panes, doorways, and corners).

A very simple way to cleanse your space is with a selenite crystal. All you have to do is set it in the center of your room for at least five minutes (maybe a little longer for larger spaces). Then you can come back to a cleansed space without exerting too much energy.

Once you have cleansed the room and you're starting from a place of neutral energy, you may want to take it a step further and charge your space with energy to match the intention of your spell.

Charging a space is a simple concept and I'm sure you'd done it many times throughout your life without even knowing.

Have you ever hosted a birthday party? What did you do? Maybe you turned on some fun, high-energy music. You might have put up streamers, balloons or some kind of eye-catching decorations to give the room a celebratory feeling. You could plan for all the food and drinks match the joyful, vibrant mood of the party—maybe you use colorful plates or add fun garnishes to the drinks.

All of those things are examples of how we intuitively "charge" a space to make it feel fun and celebratory in honor of someone's birthday.

Think about that when you want to charge your own space. Identify what kind of energy your spell needs. For example, you'll want to make the space feel warm, cozy, and romantic for a love spell. You might choose to put on some love songs, dim the lights, and spray your favorite perfume in the room.

If you're performing a spell to increase your psychic abilities, you'll want to cultivate the energy of quiet, peaceful meditation. You might choose to diffuse your favorite essential oil into the air (or use one that is associated with psychic awareness like jasmine or rose oil). Put on some soothing instrumental music. Drink a cup of tea and breath in the steam. Lavender, dandelion or chamomile are great for this intention.

The alternative to cleansing and charging your space is to find a space that already holds the energy you desire for your spellwork. To do this, simply make a list of all the places that come to mind when you think of your intention.

For a money spell, I mentioned how I did my

spells in the forest. Other places that could be ideal for this might be: in a beautiful hotel room, in a bathtub filled with rose petals and bubbles, at the kitchen table as you munch on a delicious cheese plate, in a big, sprawling art museum, or in front of a gorgeous fountain.

Your Magical Tools Were Holding Conflicting Energy.

All those candles, cauldrons, incense cones, mason jars, and crystals you have in your magical collection all tend to hold onto energy. Even magical tools that you buy brand new will come to you with an assortment of energy attached. Think about all the different hands, surfaces, rooms, vehicles, and boxes your magical merchandise has gone through to get to you. That's quite a mixture. When you're using those tools, you're bringing all of that energy into your spellwork. Sometimes it's a good thing—if the energy is a match. Oftentimes, it won't be a match. It will be a hodgepodge of random people's hopes and dreams, moods, and thoughts. That's a lot of energy from a lot of different sources.

As for the magical tools you had for a while, you

may want to cleanse those, too. They'll be holding the energy of whatever spells you've been using them to perform. Your cauldron that you filled with water and gazed into for scrying will still hold that dreamy sort of energy. That might not be what you want for your confidence spell or your home blessing spells—or maybe it is. You can decide!

Likewise, if you wanted to use that cauldron to diffuse essential oil for a divination spell, you may very well want to make use of that lingering scrying energy rather than wiping it clean. Even your collection of crystals, which many witches believe hold onto their own energy, could benefit from a cleansing—especially if you hold that crystal and sense something feels a little off or you aren't seeing the results of your spell.

You may also choose to cleanse your second hand tools—things you pick up at thrift shops, garage sales or are given to you by friends. They will likely have that hodgepodge energy similar to your newly purchased tools, except these objects might have been collecting energy for years, or decades!

Homemade magical tools can also hold conflicting energy and add resistance to your spells. Some witches enjoy making their own altar cloths, divination cards, runes, and candles. Be mindful that the energy you are feeling WHILE YOU ARE CREATING YOUR TOOLS will seep into the tool.

If you're using magical tools found in nature, they will likely already hold compatible energy. Rocks, feathers, leaves, and herbs from a garden can all add power to your spell. It's important to pay attention to how you collect these items though. This can sometimes make or break a spell. Check out the section below for suggestions on how to collect natural materials with love and respect.

How To Shift The Energy

Fortunately, the solution is simple! Cleanse all your magical tools before you use them so that you are starting from a "blank slate", and you don't have to overcome any conflicting or resistance energy attached to your tools! You can do this the same way you'd cleanse your magical space. Bonus points if you decide to charge your magical tool to match your intention.

To save time when cleansing your tools, you might want to gather up all your magical tools and leave them outside or by a window each new moon. That way, you'll get them cleansed all at once with minimal effort. You can also perform a white light meditation while you are surrounded by all your magical tools.

If you plan on making your own magical tools,

go for it! This is a wonderful way to forge a deep and powerful connection between you and your tools. This is especially helpful if you are a witch who feels disconnected from your intuition. Using these homemade tools may allow you to tap into your intuition easier. Only work on these tools when you are in a balanced mood. If you don't feel good as you're making your tools, take a break and come back to them when you feel better!

If you're using found objects from nature, make sure that you feel peaceful and centered when you are collecting these items for your magic. Also, you may want to "ask" the object if it would be OK with being used in your magic. To do this, hold the object in your hand, and literally ask, "Can I use you for my magic?". You can say it aloud or in your head. Then wait for an answer. Usually that answer will come as a feeling or intuitive nudge rather than spoken words. I have yet to actually hear a rock or twig talk back to me, but, hey, that's just me. I'm sure it's happened to someone. If you feel any resistance or negative energy after you ask the question, put the object back where you found it, and go looking for another item to use. Go through the same process. It's also traditional to give an offering back to nature whenever you take something. An offering could be as simple as a "thank you" or it could be something major like planting a tree.

One last thing about collecting magical tools from nature—be sure to check your local laws to make sure it's OK to take things with you.

Your Altar Wasn't Set Up Right.

I am not the kind of witch who will tell you exactly where to put all the things on your altar. There are some traditional ways to set up your altar—such as using the elements and the directions associated with those elements. Then there are items that many witches choose to include on their altars—such as items to represent the spell-caster or object of the spell, a pentagram for protection, candles to communicate their intention, a statue of a deity, and items to represent different elements.

Yes, all those things are great, and I'm totally down for a big, epic, flower-covered, candle-lit, cauldron-boiling altar.

But you don't need all that.

I personally believe that the only thing you need is an altar that matches the energy of your spell's intention. Are you seeing a pattern here? We want that energy to match!

The issue I've found with my altar is that I don't set it up in a way that makes me *feel* the energy I need to be feeling to manifest my spell. I'll put all the "right" things on the altar in the right places, but if I don't look at that altar and feel excited and happy, I'm missing out on some major spell power.

Sometimes, I'll look at my altar and feel intimidated, confused, overwhelmed, or just plain bored. You don't want that. Also keep an eye out for items that have bad memories attached to them. Even if you love that picture of you and your ex, (and even if you're TOTALLY over them) it might be adding resistance to your spellwork if you place it on your altar.

You might discover that some items have been on your altar too long and no longer fill you with joy and excitement. It's like a song you listened to too much and now you feel low-key rage whenever you hear the opening chords coming through your headphones. I create digital vision boards by collaging images in photoshop, and I'll set my "board" as the wallpaper for my laptop. I update my vision board three or four times a year, not because my vision changes, but because the images start to feel old, expected and stale. Whenever I open my laptop and don't feel excited, I know it's time to change out the pictures! I do the same thing with my altar.

How To Shift The Energy

When you sit down in front of your altar, take a long look at all the items that you've placed on there. Notice any thoughts, feelings or emotions that come up when you do this. You might even want to pick up and hold each item to strengthen the connection between you and the item. If you feel any energy that isn't compatible with your magical intention, swap that item out for something else.

For example, if you have a rose quartz crystal on your altar to call in love, but every time you look at that pink color, you think about your new pink shirt that you spilled coffee all over last week and it makes you angry. In that situation, you're probably going to want to switch out that crystal. I know, I know, rose quartz is perfect for calling in love, but if it's causing you unwanted emotions, it's probably not going to give you the desired result for your spell.

I'll share another example about when I use tarot cards on my altar. I love the illustrations on the cards and I'll often use them on my altar. However, I will often use cards that are not traditionally associated with my intention. For example, I'll use the Empress card for psychic enhancement spells. The Empress traditionally holds the energy of abundance, fertility, and sensuality. The High Priestess or the Hermit held more psychic energy, but I just love that Empress card. She's so beautiful and goddess-like. It makes me feel connected to that wild, magical part of myself when I see the Empress card on my altar. That makes me feel magical and spiritual more than the other cards.

You'll know you have the right objects (for you) on your altar when you look at each item and feel good and excited for your desire to manifest.

Next, make sure that the placement of the items on your altar are aesthetically pleasing to you. If you like having a lot of items on your altar, load it up, but stop just before it starts to feel cluttered. If you're a minimalist, choose three or four items, and place them exactly how you want.

Also, if you don't feel like using an altar at all for your spell, don't use it! Perform your magical visualization or repeat your incantation as you take a walk around your neighborhood or while you sip coffee at your local cafe.

You do you, powerful witch!

You Wore The Wrong Clothes.

This one is super nit-picky, but you and I both know that what you wear affects your mood, your emotions, and your energy.

To go a step further, if your clothing affects your energy, *and* that energy is powering your spell, you'll want to make sure your clothing makes you feel the way you expect to feel once your spell has manifested.

Think about how you feel when you show up underdressed to a party. Everyone is wearing sparkling dresses and smart-looking cufflinks, and you're rocking jeans and a t-shirt. Many people in that situation would feel out of place and maybe a little embarrassed. I certainly would. The reason for that is because there is a huge gap between the level of dressiness of your outfit compared to the rest of the partygoers.

Yes, you got it. I'm talking about that mismatched energy again.

In the same way, what you wear when you're spellcasting may affect the quality of energy you're using to power your spell. You may find it beneficial to wear something that feels expensive and luxurious if you're casting a money spell, or wear some fancy underwear if you're performing a love spell. If you're doing a home blessing spell, try wearing something cozy that you'll wear on a quiet evening on the couch or an outfit you'd wear while hosting a dinner party. If you're performing a confidence spell, wear something that makes you feel confident. For a psychic awareness spell, wear something that feels magical and otherworldly.

If you don't want to wear a whole spell-themed outfit, that's OK, too. I usually wear yoga pants and tank tops while spellcasting because I feel cute and comfortable in them. However, I will still add one or two details to put myself in the mood of my desired outcome. I'll wear a pretty ring or bracelet for a money spell, or I'll use a hair tie in a color that I associated with my intention (such as green for money, purple for strengthening my connection to the spirit realm, yellow for happiness and success, etc).

Some witches want to wear something to feel powerful when they are spellcasting. This is a great thing to do if you tend to second guess your own power. Maybe for you that means dressing up in a purple velvet cape, wearing all black, or not wearing anything at all! No matter what it is, be intentional about it. If you're a witch who practices with one or more witches, you might all decide to coordinate outfits in order to feel a strong sense of unity and connection. Dressing in similar colors, costumes, or wearing matching necklaces can help you focus on the idea that all your powers are being combined to achieve one magical outcome.

How To Shift The Energy

Before you begin your spell, think about what your life will be like once your spell has manifested. What will you be wearing? How will your hair look? Will you wear jewelry? What kind of shoes will you be walking around in? Will you be spending your days at the beach, at a cafe on a laptop, chasing after kids, hiking with your family, or snuggling with your lover? Dress accordingly as if you are stepping into that ideal life right after you finish casting your spell.

Pay close attention to the EMOTIONS you feel when you select your clothing AND how you feel once you are in your spellcasting outfit. I personally believe that how you feel is more important than how you look in your clothing because feelings are incredibly powerful.

If you put on something fancy or sexy, and it makes you feel uncomfortable rather than wealthy or beautiful, try standing in front of a mirror and speaking aloud an affirmation. It can be something simple like "I am sexy," or "This is what a rich woman looks like!". (I got that second affirmation from money mindset coach Denise Duffield-Thomas.)

The witchy reason that affirmations are helpful for magic is because they allow you to hear in your own voice what you are capable of being. If you see yourself in the mirror, telling yourself you are sexy or rich or powerful—or whatever—you will internalize it and believe it on a deep energetic level. That kind of aligned energy can make a witch unstoppable.

If you still don't feel good in your chosen outfit after doing your affirmations, do not beat yourself up. Let me repeat that—do not ever beat yourself up, you wonderful, beautiful, powerful witch. Don't do that.

Simply, change your clothes into something that

makes you feel good—regardless of how it matches the intention of your spell. Feeling good matches the vibration of basically every intention. It's all-purpose. Go for that feeling above all.

You Didn't Take Enough Action After Your Spell.

I was dating this guy who wanted to be a full-time writer so badly! He had a Master's in creative writing. He wrote short stories and had even completed a couple full-length novels. He talked about being a famous writer all the time. He'd go to book signings and dream about the day people would come to see him in their local bookstore.

Was he capable of being a full-time published writer? Yes. Totally. I believe most people are more than capable of achieving that. You don't have to be a genius. You just have to know how to communicate with words.

You'd think the next logical step for my boyfriend would be to sit down and research literary agents that represent his type of fiction, right?

Except he never took the next step. He never typed up a query letter. He never emailed agents. He never did anything with his book for years.

I remembered one time when his car broke down, he was complaining to me about how life was too hard and he'd never be a full time writer and he would be broke his whole life, blah, blah, blah.

In his defense, he was kind of having a rough time of it and I'm not making light of his feelings.

Still, I remember him saying something like, "Why won't God help me become a published novelist?"

And to that, I said, "Did you ever stop to think that maybe there's a spiritual reason that you have a girlfriend who knows about indie publishing, manuscript formatting, and cover design? Maybe indie publishing is the way to make this long-held dream of yours a reality!"

I've seen a lot of witches and well-meaning spiritual teachers say, "You don't have to take any action! Let your desire flow towards you!"

I do believe that to some degree. Remember when I mentioned in the beginning how there's emerging research about meditation actually changing your body? BUT even in that instance, action *was* taken—daily meditation.

We are all in our physical bodies, currently living on planet earth. Because of that, sometimes the quickest, most easeful path to our desires is through action.

If you see something that sounds like it will get you one baby step closer to your magical outcome, TAKE IT. That opportunity could be your spell manifesting in just the right way for you!

I, personally, have never lost weight or toned muscles through meditation alone, but I have cast a spell to help me get a healthy, toned body full of energy. After that particular spell, I noticed a flyer arrive in the mail advertising a beautiful new gym right down the street. Then I decided I wanted a personal trainer to help me learn how to lift weights, but I couldn't afford it. I noticed that the gym had several group fitness classes that focused on barbell and kettlebell classes—all included with the gym membership. Then, because the classes were at certain times, I had to plan my writing time, family/social time, and meals around my classes.

This forced me to be consistent in many different areas of my life, and my overall quality of life improved.

Would my spell have manifested if I hadn't joined the gym? Maybe. In my experience, the universe gives you a few chances if you miss out on the first opportunity. But I do believe that for that spell to work, you have to meet the universe halfway and make some lifestyle changes.

I also believe that consistency is KEY in

bringing about your desired magical outcome. If I stopped moving my body on a regular basis, I'd be breaking my deal with the universe and I'd backslide into my old energy of not taking my fitness seriously.

Look at nature for proof of this. Plants grow if they are cared for with proper sunlight and consistent watering. The lunar phases move from new moon to full moon and back again—consistent over the years, decades, and centuries. Same with the sun rising and setting. Consistency is everywhere in nature, and if you are on the lookout for it, you'll see it in your relationships, your career, sometimes even in your own body.

That's not to say it's good to force yourself to do something that feels wrong, fear-based, or something that just isn't you. Again, look to nature. Some plants need water everyday. Others need it once a week or even once a month. You don't have to conform to someone else's routine if it isn't working for you.

As an indie writer, I do this to myself a lot. I push myself to put in more hours than what I can comfortably do each day, and it starts to make me feel drained mentally, physically, and emotionally. There's no way I can be consistent on that kind of schedule for long. Maybe it works for other people, but not this writer!

Slow and steady, baby.

What's your pace? What can you be consistent with that gets you one step closer to your spell?

When it comes to taking action to make steps towards your magical outcome, you want to keep two things in mind:

-Take the right action, something that feels like a growth opportunity sent by the universe. I like to call this "taking aligned action".

-Do those actions at a pace that suits who you are a witch, a human, and a spiritual being.

To go back to my boyfriend who wanted to be a novelist, he did end up indie publishing. We designed him a nice cover, formatted the book, and set up a website. And he sold exactly seven copies.

Why?

Because he didn't market the book, he didn't tell people about it, and he didn't follow it up with another book to keep his momentum going.

Turned out, he didn't want to be a writer the same way I did, and because of that, he didn't have the motivation to be consistent with indie publishing. It didn't suit his personality or desires. We found out during the process of indie publishing that my boyfriend really did prefer going the traditional publishing route.

Who knows, maybe if he had continued down the path of indie publishing, a traditional publishing house would have offered him a book deal. It's happened to me, and many other indie authors.

But the indie way didn't suit my BF, and he honored that by not moving forward on that path.

I don't know what he's up to not, but I hope he's writing stories and sending them out to agents. Those small actions could be all he needed to open up the flow of energy and receive all that he's been desiring.

How To Shift The Energy

The moment you finish your spell, start looking for opportunities that get yourself one step closer to your desired outcome. The universe, your deities, your inner wisdom, or whatever you believe in will constantly be sending little clues in your direction.

These signs could be:

-Small wins or successes

-Encouraging words from others

-Seeing what you desire show up for other people in your life

-Feeling good

-Noticing synchronicities, or signs that mean something to you that aren't directly connected to anything—things that seem random, but YOU can see the meaning.

-Opportunities showing up, sometimes out of nowhere

-Noticing other areas of your life improving (such as you performed a money spell, but your relationship with your children improved).

You Didn't Word Your Spell Correctly.

I've talked about how to write effective magical spells in my other book, *How to Become a Witch*, but I'll give you the quick and dirty version here.

Basically, words are powerful. When you speak something in your mind or aloud, you are manifesting a statement.

"I am powerful."

"I am beautiful."

"I am an internationally-known writer."

"My screenplay sells for $100,000."

"My house is steps away from the ocean and I fall asleep listening to the waves each night."

These are all examples of spells that follow my three guidelines. As someone who has studied and experimented with the Law of Attraction, personal development, and witchcraft, I've found that my spells manifest best if I write my spell or intention in this format.

Here are my tips:

1. Your intention should be written or spoken in the first person (if the spell is meant to manifest something for yourself).

The reason for this is because I want to be as clear as possible that this is *my* spell and I, the spellcaster, am the one who is sending out this desire so that it may manifest in *my* life.

2. Your intention should be written or spoken in the present tense (not future tense).

This is important because if you say "I *will* sell my screenplay for $100,000", then your spell will always hold the energy of you receiving this desire *in the future*. When you say, "I will", that implies you don't currently have your desire. Though I do think it's important to acknowledge the present situation, I believe that when you are actively casting a spell you should shift your energy AS MUCH AS POSSIBLE to the energy you will feel and experience once the desire has manifested. To do this, it helps to speak the intention as if it is *currently manifesting*.

(We'll get more into this concept in the second part of the book where I talk about internal factors that affect your spell.)

3. The focus on your intention needs to be on the positive, not the negative.

This goes along with the concept that the universe is constantly expanding.

To do make your intuition positive-focused, think about what you'll *gain* from your spell, not what you'll *lose*.

Positive-Focused Intention: "I walk along the beach in a bikini and I smile as I notice people checking out and admiring my body." This is an intention where the focus is on attracting positive attention, feeling good in your skin, and enjoying your time at the beach.

Negative-Focused Intention: "I lose twenty-five pounds so I can look good in my bikini." This statement, although it follows the other guidelines, is focusing on losing weight—LOSING being the key word. "Lose", "decrease", "zero", and "no" are all negative-focused words that can add unnecessary resistance to your spells. I'm not saying don't use them in conversation, but I am saying that these kinds of words might cause your spells to manifest slower (or not at all).

Another example I hear a lot is witches casting spells with the intention, "I am debt-free". The focus with this intention is on debt—a negative focus. Instead try something like, "I have more than enough money to cover all of my bills and my savings account grows every day."

Note: You might be wondering why these intentions aren't written in rhymes like traditional spells—sometimes called incantations. The reason I teach this is because I find that having my intention be close to the way I normally speak makes me feel a stronger connection to it.

Historically, spells were shared from witch to witch through short, easy-to-remember rhymes, poems, or songs. Because witchcraft was highly controversial in those times (sometimes even considered a crime), witches chose not to write their spells down to keep from getting caught practicing magic.

If you want to write a spell that rhymes, go for it. See if it makes you feel witchy and powerful. If I ever cast a spell with a rhyme, I will still follow those three guidelines.

I'd also like to encourage you to try writing you own spells. I almost always create my own intentions and incantations, rather than using spells out of books. I think that the words I put together come from a deep magical place inside of me—my inner wisdom. I think we are all born with powers and ancient knowledge, and writing spells is a way to directly tap into that part of ourselves. If you've never tried writing your own spells, give it a try and see what kind of results you get!

How To Shift The Energy

If you suspect your intention isn't as powerful as it could be, take a moment to write it out. Examine it using the three guidelines I've shared here, and see if you can revise it.

Then speak the intention aloud and see how it makes you feel. Do you feel excited? Happy? Optimistic? That's when you know you've got a winner.

You Told Someone About Your Spell And They Reacted Negatively.

You know how this goes. You cast a spell. You're so excited because you can just FEEL the energy moving towards you. You've just *know* you're going to get exactly what you want.

Then you tell your best friend about your desire, and instead of being excited, they start telling you all the reasons why you won't (or shouldn't) get what you want.

Immediately, you lose confidence in yourself and your magic. This can be a reason your spell didn't manifest.

It's important to remember in these situations that the reactions of others aren't personal. They probably have absolutely nothing to do with you.

In my experience when people react negatively to my goals, it's because of these reasons:

1. They are used to seeing me a certain way, and if I tell them about my desire, it forces them to see me in a new way.

For example, if you're single, and you tell your friend that you cast a love spell to meet your next romantic partner, they might not be used to thinking of you as anything other than their "single friend". They might react negatively because they are having a hard time wrapping their mind around your "new identity".

2. The second reason is that people who love us don't necessarily want what's best for us. They want what's SAFEST for us. That's because they don't want to see us disappointed, hurt, or in any kind of a risky situation. A lot of times, growth requires risk. Most spells cause you to change and grow. Growth is scary. Therefore, telling your friends about your spells might scare them.

Though it's helpful to get support from your loved ones, it can also totally take the wind out of your sails if they have negative things to say. Don't put yourself in a situation like this—especially if you are in the very early stages of manifesting your spells. You don't need any extra hate when your desire is just starting to grow.

How To Shift The Energy

Don't tell your friends, family, or ANYONE about your spell unless you are prepared for their reaction. You can always tell everyone *after* your spell has manifested. That way they have time to wrap their minds around the new you.

If you do choose to tell people about your spell, and they are negative, don't let it get you down. Remind yourself that the person's reaction is because of THEIR mindset and it has absolutely nothing to do with you. Let go of any unhelpful energy. You know what's best for you.

You Didn't Plan For Success.

Sometimes the universe (or your higher powers, personal deities, or whatever you believe in) wants to deliver the ideal outcome of your spell to you, but it can't because there's no place for it in your life.

Let's say you cast a spell to attract your true love. I'd invite you to ask yourself this question: If your true love showed up today, would you be ready for them?

Is your life set up to accommodate this new person? Is your home tidied up so you can have your true love over for evening cuddle times? Do you take time off from work each week for relaxing and socializing with this potential lover? Do you have pretty clothes to wear so you feel sexy around your true love?

Just because you've cast the spell, doesn't mean

you're done with the magic. There's always more you can do to open up that flow of energy and invite your desire into your life.

If you want to manifest a three month trip to France, look for small ways you can prep yourself for this trip even if you have absolutely no idea how something like that could manifest. Take some french classes. Pull your suitcase out of your closet. Figure out how to ask your boss to let you work remotely for three months. Look into getting a cat sitter for your fur baby. Tell your friends and family what you'd like to do (if you think they'll be supportive).

The more space you make in your life for your desire to manifest, the more likely it will manifest. Give it a try for yourself. It works like a charm for me.

☆

How To Shift The Energy

In the days after your spell, think about how that new desire would fit into your life. Then start making little changes. With each change you make, your energy will become more and more aligned to the energy of your desire. Think of this work as a continuation of your spell.

INTERNAL REASONS
YOUR SPELL
DIDN'T WORK

You Didn't Ground Yourself First.

G rounding is a magical process that doesn't get the attention it deserves. As a witch, you spend a lot of time working with energy. This energy can come from every corner of the universe—from both the physical world *and* the spiritual world.

All of that energy can be a lot to manage.

Think about how you feel when you go to a theme park. There's so much to see and do. You eat some funnel cake. You joke around with your friends and family while standing in line for rides. You throw darts at balloons and win a huge Winnie the Pooh. You have a wonderful fun-filled day.

Then you go home, rest, and get back to your daily routine.

Now imagine if you spent every day for an entire month at that theme park—all day eating hot dogs and cotton candy, playing the games and riding the rides.

How do you think you'd feel after that?

You'd probably never, ever want to step foot in a theme park for the rest of your life.

That's kind of what you are doing to your energy when you cast spell after spell without taking time to ground yourself and reset your energy. Yes, casting spells is fun, and yes, sometimes it makes you feel better emotionally and energetically—just like spending the day at the theme park.

But if you cast a spell and you're feeling all amped up from the various energies of your day, you might be adding resistance to your spell. Taking time to ground yourself can raise the effectiveness of almost any magical spell.

> Note: There are a few types of spells that you wouldn't want to ground yourself before trying—astral projection, for example. For something like that, you want to feel all floaty and buzzing with energy.

☆

How To Shift The Energy

There are many different ways to ground yourself. Most of the time, you already know what to do

WHY DIDN'T MY SPELL WORK?

when you feel uncomfortable physically, mentally, or emotionally.

The first step to grounding is to figure out what you need to make yourself feel better in that moment. There's no need to make this more complicated than it needs to be.

If you're hungry, eat something. If you're thirsty, get something to drink. If you need a nap, go to bed. If you have a headache, treat it the way you normally would like taking medication or using a home remedy.

A simple meditation I recommend for grounding yourself is to stand with both feet on the ground (or sit if that's more comfortable) and visualize pink roots sprouting from your feet going into the ground. In your mind's eye, see those roots growing deeper and deeper into the ground until they connect with the energetic center of the earth. Take a few minutes to absorb that peaceful energy. If you have too much energy and need to release some, you can send any excess energy through your roots down into the earth. When you feel relaxed and balanced, you can open your eyes and begin your witchcraft.

You Weren't Feeling Your Best On The Day You Cast Your Spell.

There are many reasons why you might not be feeling that great every moment of every day. Welcome to being human. We all have good days and bad days. We all get sick, get tired, get worn down, get stressed—you name it. We experience disappointments, loss, physical and mental ailments, everyday annoyances, and misunderstandings with loved ones. Our houses get messy, our cars break down, our dogs throw up on the carpeting, our kids act out in school—and all of these things affect our energy.

Some of these issues are temporary upsets, and others are long-term issues. I've talked to witches who are dealing with on-going health issues, such as chronic pain and major depressive disorder.

If you are dealing with an ongoing issue that affects how you feel most of the time—like chronic pain or depression—you can still MOST DEFINITELY perform powerful magic. I've been treated for (and am STILL being treated for) depression. I refuse to let depression stop me from blossoming as a witch.

How To Shift The Energy

I'm not going to tell you to plaster on a fake smile and proclaim, "I FEEL GREAT!". That's not going to do you any good to ignore your pain. In fact, it might make you feel even worse. The best way I know how to shift your energy when you're not feeling that great is to take baby steps to make yourself feel slightly better.

There's got to be *something* you can do to make yourself feel just a teeny-tiny bit better. Brainstorm a list of ways to do this and don't rule anything out.

Maybe you need a chocolate bar, a Netflix marathon, a few breaths of fresh air, a moment of mediation, a hug from a loved one, or a walk with your dog.

Right now, there is something that can boost you one notch higher, and that will most certainly have a positive impact on your spell. Doing things like this is also a form of self-care—something that is an important part of a witch's life. Self-care, no matter what it is, will always increase your power.

Also, sometimes the best option is to wait until tomorrow to cast your spell. As Poet Robert Frost says, "The best way out is always through." There is no shame in simply sitting in your pain until it passes.

After my really bad heartbreak (and spiritual crisis) I spent a month or so watching all eight seasons of *The Vampire Diaries*. Then, right after that, I had the idea to start publishing books—which is what took my business to the next level. Was it an indulgent waste of time to watch 171 episodes of a paranormal teen soap? Not for me it wasn't it. Those two brooding Salvatore vampires were exactly what I needed to process my heartache.

The heart wants what the heart wants, and giving that to yourself—silly as it sounds—can bring about magic you'd never imagine possible.

When you're going through a dark time, you can continue to practice your magic, *or* you take a break.

On days you don't feel up for casting a big spell, you can perform simple magical acts throughout your day like saying hello to the elements when you're drinking tea or carrying your favorite crystal around in your pocket.

You Got Upset When Someone Else Got What You Desire.

You cleansed your magical tools, you wrote your intention perfectly, you performed your spell to manifest your dream home. You even took some aligned action to meet the universe halfway, such as contacting realtors and researching different neighborhoods.

And then...

Your best friend closed on her dream home—totally out of the blue.

All the while, you're tapping your foot, being like, "Um, why did *she* get that and not me? Also, why the heck was it *so easy* for her?"

Believe it or not, that kind of thinking adds resistance to your magic. Personally, I've found that the more jealous I am of other people's accomplishments, the longer it takes for my own spells to work.

For me, jealousy stems from the belief that there is not enough to go around—that there is limited money, limited opportunities, and limited gifts that get passed out.

This is not how this universe works.

For starters, the universe is constantly expanding. There is abundance all around us. New money is printed every day, and new forms of currency are being invented all the time. New people are being born all over the world. That means there are always new people to meet, to be friends with, to sell things to, and to buy things from.

Chew on that for a minute, and say it with me, "The universe is abundant. The universe is unlimited."

If you can internalize that radical idea, then you are going to see magic flowing to you like never before. It may even help you let go of the jealousy that has been energetically weighing you down.

If you believe that there is more than enough to go around, that the universe is plentiful, magical and always expanding, then why would you feel anything by pure joy when your friend gets what you want? Your friend getting *her* dream house has absolutely no negative impact on you getting *your* dream house. It's the same with anything else. Your neighbor getting a sweet Mustang convertible, won't stop you from getting your own awesome Mustang convertible. Your neighbor may share some car buying tips with you.

In fact, I believe that when you start to see *your* spells manifesting in other people's lives, that means your personal manifestation is coming your way very soon. Spells manifest because of aligned energy, and if someone close to you manifests your desire, it means that aligned energy is hovering around you.

There's also something called social modeling which is the idea that if you see someone similar to you achieving something, your subconscious accepts that it's possible for you AND you'll start to make tiny behavior changes to achieve that same thing.

How To Shift The Energy

I want to stress the fact that we cannot control our feelings. We *feel* them. They move through us whether we want them to or not. Then eventually, they fade and new feelings take their place.

If you DO notice that you're feeling jealous:

- Congratulate yourself for being self-aware enough to notice that you're jealous. That's a huge step.

- Do not beat yourself up for feeling jealous. It's natural, and it is based on a scarcity mindset that humans developed in caveman days for purposes of survival. There is nothing wrong with you for feeling jealous.
- Remind yourself that there is no need for you to feel jealous in this abundant universe.
- Tell yourself, "The universe is abundant. The universe is limitless."
- Celebrate other's people's success.
- Know that yours is on the way.
- Be on the lookout for opportunities that get you closer to your desire

You Didn't Ask For Enough (Or You Asked For Too Much).

Whatever outcome you're trying to achieve with your magic, you want that desire to feel big and exciting.

Why?

Because emotions super-charge your spells. When you think about your desire, the emotions that accompany those thoughts will continue to power your spell—even when you're not actively performing the spell at your altar (or wherever you do your magic).

If your magical intention wasn't big and bold enough, you might not feel *any* emotion when you think about it. If that's the case, you're missing on a major source of power inside of you.

For example, if your magical intention is "I sell one product on Etsy", and when you think about that intention you are kind of "eh" about it, that "eh" energy might create some resistance.

Try making the intention bigger. For example: "I make $100 on Etsy in one week". That might excite you more. If it doesn't, keep making that intention bigger.

On the flip side, if you cast a spell with the intention, "I make $100,000 on Etsy in one week" and you haven't made your first sale yet, your emotions might be working against your magic.

The reason for this is because you might not believe a spell like this is possible. Maybe consciously, you believe it's possible, but all the while your subconscious is like, "Yeah right. Not happening anytime soon!"

That's when you know that intention isn't quite aligned to your emotions.

☆

How To Shift The Energy

Speak your intention aloud. Then journal about the emotions, thoughts, and images that come to mind immediately after. If you're feeling things **like excitement, exhilaration, expansion, adventure, contentment, joy, or anything along those lines**, **you've probably chosen an intention that is just right for your**

current energy. If you feel a little bit of fear as well, that's totally fine. A *little* fear is good. People usually feel slightly freaked out when they are expanding into new territory or growing in new ways.

If you speak your intention and you feel bored, indifferent, annoyed, tired, or uninspired, you've probably selected an intention that is either too small for you, or it isn't exactly what your heart wants. Maybe the desire is something you think you're "supposed" to do or something you think will please someone else. These sorts of intentions are hard to manifest through magic because your heart's not in it.

If you speak your intention and you feel panicked, terrified, dizzy, hot, overwhelmed, hopeless, or depressed, you may have chosen an intention that is too big for your current energy. This doesn't mean you won't ever manifest this big goal. It just means that your subconscious hasn't fully gotten on board yet. It's likely that some part of you doesn't believe this desire is attainable for you, and those uncomfortable emotions you're feeling are push-back from your subconscious. Consider breaking up your big goal into small parts and casting a spell for the first part. Then once that first part has manifested, try casting a spell for the second part of the goal.

Your Magical Intention Was Too Specific.

Once I cast a spell to get what I thought was my DREAM JOB. It was a position as the inventory manager at a well-known metaphysical shop. The pay was good and so were the benefits. I was also totally qualified because I had experience designing and selling my oracle deck. I went through several interviews, and it sounded like I was going to get the job.

I was so excited. I burned candles, did some visualizations, and wrote down my intention several times a day to magically draw this job closer to me. In my mind, I had that job.

But after the third interview, they never got back to me—not even an email saying they filled the position like they promised. I felt totally crushed, embarrassed, played-with, and powerless.

If I was such a powerful witch, why couldn't I

manifest this awesome job that was totally suited for me?

I sobbed on the phone to my mom, my friends, and anyone who would listen—not just because I didn't get the job that felt like THE job, but also because my confidence as a witch took a big hit.

Then a few weeks later, I saw a job on Facebook looking for someone to be a cashier at a wine shop. I didn't know much about wine, but the shop looked cute and it was close to my house. A bunch of people responded to the post, but the manager emailed me back with a job offer. No interview necessary.

The job turned out to be PERFECT for me. It covered all my bills, had flexible hours, and NO ONE EVER CAME IN. I basically got to be on my laptop all day at the shop, working on my online business and writing books. I wrote three novels while on the clock at that job, and my manager was totally cool with it!

Looking back, I can honestly say it was the job I needed at that point in my life. Everyday as I opened that little neighborhood shop, I thanked the universe for keeping me from getting that full-time job at the metaphysical shop. There was no way I would have been able to write three full-length novels at any other job—especially not a busy retail store during the holidays. No. Freaking. Way.

How To Shift The Energy

So the takeaway here is when you get *too* specific, and you give the universe only ONE SINGLE way to fulfill your spell, that spell might not work.

I did end up with a fantastic job, but I could have saved myself a lot of emotional pain if I'd made my spell less specific. Rather than my intention being, "I am the inventory manager of Crystal Magic", I should have cast a spell with the intention, "I work a job that perfectly supports my lifestyle and is suited to my overall desire to be an entrepreneur and writer."

Both intentions are specific, but the second one is more open-ended and invites the universe to deliver the absolute best outcome.

If I *choose* to be specific with my spells, I'll now add the phase, "This or better", meaning that though I believe this is what I want, I also trust the universe (or my personal deities, God, whatever) to bring me what I want even if I can't imagine what that is.

Your Magical Intention Was Not Specific Enough.

I know we just got done talking about why you shouldn't make your spell so specific to the point where it limits the ways the universe can deliver your desired outcome.

However, you also don't want to be too vague with your intention. A lot of times this happens when witches mistake affirmations for magical intentions or incantations.

Affirmations are statements that you speak aloud to yourself in order to shift your energy. People often speak their affirmations in the mirror first thing in the morning, or they'll set reminders on their phone and speak these statements throughout the day to keep their energy buoyant.

Here are some examples of common money affirmations:

"I receive money."

"I am rich."

"Money flows to me."

"I am a money magnet."

These are all wonderful, powerful, energy-shifting statements, but personally, I don't use statements like this when I'm casting spells. I make my magical intentions a bit more specific.

The reason for this is because you want to make sure you give the universe some further guidance so it doesn't send you something you don't want.

For example: I used the affirmation, "Money flows to me," for one of the first money spells I cast. At the time, I was working remotely for a publishing company and absolutely hated it. It was a lot of work for not much pay, and my boss constantly messaged me at all hours with more work for me to do. I even had work to do on Christmas.

I cast the money spell because I wanted to quit this job and become a full-time entrepreneur. I assumed the universe would respond by sending me customers to buy my products through my new business.

This didn't happen. Instead, almost immediately after I cast my spell, I got offered a raise at the job I HATED.

Ugh.

A better intention to use in that situation would have been, "Money flows to me through my entrepreneurial efforts." An intention like that is specific enough to make sure I get what I want, but it's also open-ended enough so that the universe can make sure I receive my desire in the best, most magical, most aligned way possible.

How To Shift The Energy

Look over your intention for your spell and brainstorm all the ways the universe might bring you your desire. Put check marks by the ways that you would appreciate. Then rewrite your intention so that it is more clear about how you want that desire to manifest.

You Made Excuses For Why You Can't Manifest Your Spell.

This is one of the big energetic blocks a lot of people develop when their spells don't work.

They start to make excuses for why they didn't get something. They get into a victim mentality. Sometimes, they talk themselves out of wanting the thing in the first place.

This "excuse mindset" can be subtle or overt. Sometimes you won't even notice you're doing it, which is why it's really important to pay attention to your thoughts and feelings before, during and after your spellwork.

Once I was watching a documentary about the woman who lost her arm from a shark attack. The movie was inspiring and I was especially interested in the woman's mindset. Despite losing her arm at a young age, she never thought of herself being at any sort of disadvantage. Not only was she going to keep surfing, this girl was still determined to go pro.

She went on to become one of the most famous surfers in the world.

I believe that her powerful mindset is a big reason she was able to be so successful, and mindset it a big part of witchcraft.

The strange thing is that, as I was watching this documentary, I began comparing her life to my life and listing out all the external reasons this woman was destined to succeed.

My mental list looked something like this:

-She had parents who encouraged her to take risks and taught her to manage her fears.

-She was pretty.

-She stayed in shape and ate healthy food from a young age.

-She lived in Hawaii.

-Her parents bought her surf equipment and traveled with her for surf competitions.

-She was taught to be tenacious.

Then I began counting off all my disadvantages. Though I had a great childhood, it was very different from the way this woman was brought up.

-My parents had a lot of fear-based beliefs. They would have never encouraged me to try a dangerous sport like surfing.

-My family didn't eat very healthy, so I was overweight as a kid.

-I felt ugly for all of my childhood, and that caused me to have low self-esteem.

-I was known as the "fat kid" and assumed that I would never be good at sports.

-I lived in Chicago where it was cold and dreary half the year.

On and on, my excuses went.

Without even realizing it on a conscious level, I drew the conclusion that because my upbringing was not like this woman's, *she* had all these advantages over me that set her up for success.

This, my witchy friend, is the mindset block that can create massive resistance to your spells.

As soon as I caught myself thinking that thought, I gave myself a mental slap.

Had I seriously just thought that this woman had a better chance at becoming a a pro surfer than me?

I had to consciously shift my thinking so that I snapped out of this ridiculous excuse-making mindset.

I reminded myself that this woman *lost an arm in a shark attack* as a child, and she had to overcome a ton of physical, mental and emotional issues to achieve her dream. I have both of my arms, and I did not live through a traumatic shark attack. How could I think for one second that I was disadvantaged?

All those "reasons" I gave for why *I* was disadvantaged were straight-up excuses. **This is a defense mechanism. We create those excuses to protect ourselves from disappointment. We don't want to go for something, not get it, and feel like huge losers.**

Instead we create perfectly "rational" reasons for why the thing we want was really out of our reach all along.

If I was to perform a spell in that headspace of "I'm disadvantaged", than that energy would affect my spell.

For example, if I perform a spell to get a job, and all the while I'm making excuses for why I'm not qualified for this job—that might have an impact on my spell's outcome. I recommend doing everything you can to get yourself out of that "disadvantaged" energy before you begin your spell-casting.

How To Shift The Energy

Unless you examine your thoughts, feelings, and energy closely, you might not know you are sending out conflicting energies when you're performing your spell. That's the tricky thing about this one.

Here's a simple journaling mediation I've

done to energetically clear out any excuses I've been holding onto unknowingly.

Step One: Think about your desired outcome of the spell.

Step Two: Pick someone you know who is living that same outcome that you desire from your spell.

Step Three: Make a list about all the reasons why that person has the "thing" you are magically manifesting.

Step Four: Make a list with all the reasons why it's harder for you than it is for that person to manifest that same outcome. Yes, you read that right. I want you to get all of those resistance-causing thoughts out of your subconscious and onto the paper.

Step Five: Go through each of those reasons from the second list and journal about how why that's an excuse.

Step Six: If you want to make this a mini spell, write down each of these excuses from your second list on slips of paper (or draw a sigil or picture to represent each excuse) and burn them in a cauldron or fireproof container.

For Example:

Step One: Let's say my intention is to manifest the sale of my Christmas-themed romance screenplay. (That's something I'm personally manifesting right now.)

Step Two: There's a romance novelist I read about online who turned her book into a screenplay and Hallmark made it into a movie.

Step Three: Here's my first list—the reasons why this person is uniquely set up for success already.

-She is traditionally published.

-She has a husband who supports her financially

-She has a writing coach.

-She's written many other romance novels.

-She has a literary agent.

I'm going to stop right here and comment on how silly these reasons all sound now that I'm writing them out. However, the fact that I was able to jot those down so quickly tells me they've been taking up space in my subconscious.

Step Four: Now I'll make my second list of reasons why it will be harder for me than for that other lady to manifest this desire.

-I've never written a romance novel before.

-I couldn't get a literary agent in the past to a traditional publishing deal.

-I have to support myself financially while I take time to write this screenplay.

-I've only been making money fiction writing for a couple years.

Think about this: all of these excuses were lurking around in my energy field, clogging up my magical energy, subtly lowering the effectiveness of my spell. Who needs that? Not this witch!

Step Five: Finally, I'll make a list refuting all of these reasons I've created in my mind.

-Though I've never written a romance novel before, I've read a ton of them and watched many romance movies. Also, all of my novels have major romance themes, and I'm pretty good writing that kind of that stuff.

-Who cares if I don't have a literary agent or a traditional publishing deal? I make good money indie publishing and I've gotten experience writing lots of different kinds of books because I get to choose what projects I work on. Also, indie authors tend to write faster and publish more frequently than traditionally published authors. Each time I complete a project, I hone my skills and improve.

-I AM supporting myself financially, and I don't see that changing anytime soon! Working on a screenplay won't change that. Also, I won't be including potential income from this screenplay in my bottom line, so writing it will feel like playtime —a creative project without any financial pressure. I can write it at my own pace.

-Even though I've only been making money writing books for a couple years, I've been paid to write for longer than that, and I've been writing without being paid for over a decade. I'm a lot more experienced than I give myself credit for!

After systematically going through all my excuses, I can see that I have so many things going for me, and there's nothing holding me back. This is the energy you want to take on while you're spellcasting.

If you find yourself making excuses for why you aren't "good enough" to get what you want, go through this exercise before you cast your next spell.

You're Scared.

It's OK to be scared. You're bound to be uncomfortable when it comes to things you're passionate about. If you aren't a little bit scared about your magical intention, you are either SUPER enlightened or you don't actually care that much about the thing you're manifesting.

The question is, what exactly is scaring you in regards to your spell?

Are you scared of the spell *not manifesting*, or are you scared of how things will change *when you do manage to manifest your spell?*

Both of these fears are equally anxiety-causing, and both have the power to complicate your magic.

Let's start with the first part—fear that your spell won't manifest. To find out if this is a fear that is weighting on you, perform this meditation.

Close your eyes and visualize what your life will look like if your spell totally flops. Think about all the aspects of your life this will affect—your daily routines, your home, your work, your relationships, your financial resources, etc. Get really deep into your visualization.

> Note: Some witches prefer to write out their visualization. Other witches like to speak it aloud like they're telling the story to someone. Others will silently let the visualization play out in their minds. If you don't know which method is most powerful to you, personally, try all three and pay attention to what feels most vivid and real to you.

Notice the fears that surface as you do this meditation. For example: If your intention is to become a six-figure entrepreneur, think about what your life will look like if you never get to that level of income. What comes up for you?

Are you scared that you'll disappoint yourself or your family who spent a lot of money on your college tuition?

Are you scared you'll be living in an apartment you hate, in a bad neighborhood for the rest of your life?

Are you scared you'll be overworked because you'll have to stay at your day job your whole life and not be able to pursue your entrepreneurial dreams?

Are you scared that if your entrepreneurial dreams don't pan out, you'll be a failure? Are you scared that no one will love or respect you if you can't manifest $100,000 a year? Are you scared that YOU will lose respect for yourself if your spell never manifests?

You see what a minefield these fears can be?

Each little fear can be obstructing the flow of your magic. As you ruminate on your fears, take note of the biggest, most upsetting fears.

Those are the ones you'll want to focus on clearing.

Now let's explore the flip side off this. Take a moment to visualize what will happen if your spell manifests exactly as you've imagined.

Maybe you're thinking, "Why the heck would I be afraid of my spell manifesting? I wouldn't be performing this spell if I didn't want it to manifest?"

Human beings are complex and contradictory. I believe almost everyone at some point in their lives has had fears of being successful.

It's time to dig around in your subconscious to see if you can dislodge some of these sneaky little fears.

I'll use the same example as before. Let's say

your magical intention is to be a 6-figure entrepreneur.

Sit down and really think about the nitty-gritty of your spell manifesting perfectly.

What will change for the better? What will change for the worse?

Are you afraid your friends and family will think you're above them? Are you afraid you'll have to pay more taxes? Are you afraid you'll manifest more problems because on some level you believe "more money, more problems"? Are you afraid you'll use your "edge" because you know you are strongly motivated by the fear of being broke or being just one step ahead of financial ruin? Are you scared of how much you'll have to work to maintain making this amount of money year after year?

These are common fears people have regarding making more money. People also have similar fears around the idea of allowing a romantic partner into their life, losing weight, and becoming a leader.

How To Shift The Energy

Gather up all your darkest fears that are related to your spell and take some time to shed light on each one.

There are a few ways you can release fears.

Here are my favorites:

-Ask the universe, your deities, your higher power, or your intuition to send you a sign to not be afraid.

Money mindset coach, Denise Duffield-Thomas often talks about how she was afraid to buy her first house. She was scared that she wouldn't be able to maintain her business and keep bringing in the money she would need to afford the house. Then on the way home from looking at the house, a huge wad of money blew RIGHT ONTO her car windshield. She had no idea where the money came from or who it belonged to. She didn't stop to collect the money or anything like that. Instead, she took that as a sign from the universe that she would be able to afford the house. She went for it, and she had zero regrets.

-Let the universe guide you to books, TV shows and movies that put your fears to rest.

I recently discovered that I had a false belief that I would be worthless if I never managed to make money from my business. I started to release that fear because of—ugh, this is so dumb, and I apologize in advance—the Fifty Shades of Grey trilogy.

If you live under a rock, like I do, I'll summarize the plot for you. An innocent college student catches the eye of this hot billionaire who is into bondage and stuff. It's a romance series, so spoiler alert—they fall in love.

After reading the books, I began to understand that money is not ultimately what attracts people to each other. If someone likes me, they'll like me with or without money, just as Christian Grey liked Ana despite her not being a rich, fancy lady. Ana is impressed by Christian's money, but it isn't what makes her love him. She loves him for his dry sense of humor, his tortured soul, and his big heart. Weirdly enough, the Fifty Shades of Grey story helped me overcome some major money blocks I'd developed. As a result, my energy shifted and I began to make more money in my business. Stories can be powerful—even romance novels!

-Pin point the specific fears and make arrangements so that you can rest easy.

For example, if you're scared of being a six-figure entrepreneur because you're afraid of messing up your taxes, consider hiring an accountant and letting them do your taxes for you.

-For all those fears that are out of your control, trust yourself to cope with whatever obstacles or issues come your way.

A lot of times our worst fears aren't actually that bad if they do happen. For example, if you mess up your taxes and you get audited, you'll probably be able to sort it out eventually. Chances are, you're not going to get thrown into a medieval dungeon if you make a mistake on your taxes. You might have to pay more money, but oftentimes you can set up a payment plan. In the process, you'll probably learn how to do your taxes correctly, so you don't run into issues in the future.

There is nothing you can't handle, witch. I'm sure of it.

-Need further proof that you've totally got this—whatever "this" is?

Look back at your past and remember all the times you got yourself out of a sticky situation. You're a lot more resourceful than you think.

You Were Too Attached To The Outcome.

When you want something so badly to the point where you feel desperate and panicky whenever you think about that desire, you can be sure that your current energy is not a match for anything other than more panic and desperation.

Even if everything else on your altar is set up beautifully and your intention is worded perfectly, you are going to have a harder time manifesting your ideal outcome if all you are feeling is desperation.

The universe can tell if you're desperate. It hold a specific vibrational frequency. You can probably sense it, too. Think about the times you've gone on dates with people.

You can tell if your date is desperate, and it's not an attractive energy. In fact, it's downright repellant.

Likewise, you probably remember times when you've been the one desperate on a date. You say things you normally wouldn't. You drop things. You laugh way too loud at jokes that aren't even funny.

I get it. I've been there, and usually, I don't get asked on a second date when I'm sending out that desperate energy.

One of my favorite podcasters, Jess Lively described this feeling of really, *really* wanting something as being "thirsty" for something. I love that term because I'm always very aware when I'm physically thirsty. I know what an intense feeling it can be.

Being "energetically" or "emotionally" thirsty is the opposite of attracting energy and it can sometimes feel just as intense as being physically thirsty.

The irony is that when you shift your energy from desperation to contentment, that's usually the moment your desire manifests.

How To Shift The Energy

There is one question I ask myself when I sense that I'm getting desperate about my magical intention.

"Could I still be happy even if I don't get what I want?"

The first answer that comes to my mind after I ask this question is usually something like, "heck no!"

But I invite you to go a little deeper.

I'm not suggesting you need to "be happy" about your spell not working. I'm asking you to mentally explore that possibility.

Would it really be that terrible if your spell didn't work? What is the absolute worse that would happen as a result? Would you stop enjoying the things you already enjoy? Would your friends abandon you? Would you get kicked out of your home? Would you fall into a long, dark depression?

Most of the time, when I think about this, the worst that would happen is that I would feel painfully disappointed.

But so what?

I've been disappointed many times in my life, and I recovered from every single disappointment. I remind myself of this whenever I start to feel that energetic "thirst".

Another way I shift my energy from desperate to content is to think of a way to energetically "quench my thirst" without needing my magical desire. For example, if I'm manifesting a dream vacation and I'm feeling desperate, I could book a much less expensive weekend trip to a beautiful location near my home. Then, no matter what happens with my spell, I know I have one fun outing to look forward to.

Here's another example: if you want to manifest a new family pet, you may consider taking your friend's dog out for a walk or volunteering at the humane society. That way you still get to be around animals—regardless of your spell's outcome.

Yes, in both of those scenarios, you'll still want your actual intention to manifest, but you probably won't feel so desperate in the meantime. This will change your energy from repellant to attractive, and the universe will take notice.

> Note: If you still feel panicky when you think about your desire, you might want to dig even deeper to see what's causing this anxiety. Are you desperate because there are areas in your life that are in bad shape?
>
> If that's the case, I recommend you get yourself some additional help immediately—the kind that comes to you through trusted friends, family, or even a mental health or medical professional. Anxiety is no joke, and there's a difference between being upset about not getting your magical desire and feeling like you're teetering on the edge of a full-fledged panic attack.
>
> Witchcraft can solve all sorts of problems, but it's not the ONLY help available to you. Get the

help you need and don't feel bad that you didn't solve your problem through "witchcraft".

As I've mentioned before, everything is connected. I've spent many hours talking out my issues with a therapist and, wow, was that time pivotal for my mental health.

Do whatever you need to do to make sure you're OK.

You Are Stuck In An Unhelpful Energetic Pattern.

Part of the reason I think I had some much trouble manifesting money earlier in my life was because I was stuck in unhelpful energetic patterns.

Usually, these energetic patterns happen because of a past experience or even childhood memories.

For me, I carried around this idea that I was bad with money. This belief came about because when I turned eighteen, my grandparents gave me my inheritance early. I immediately moved to Los Angeles and blew through thousands of dollars. I also managed to kill my credit and wrack up a bunch of debt.

From that day on, I labeled myself as someone who overspent and made terrible money decisions.

Over the next decade or so, I learned to make better money decisions and built my credit back up.

During this time, I noticed new financial opportunities appearing in my life—invites to spiritual retreats, offers for business coaching, and opportunities for bulk inventory purchases to name a few. The problem was that each opportunity required me to spend more money than what I was comfortable with, and that brought up my old belief that I was bad with money.

Each time an opportunity like this presented itself, I would be filled with fear, doubt and indecision. In my mind, I was still that person who overspent and made bad money decisions.

This is an example of a unhelpful energetic pattern.

Ironically enough, my fear of being bad with many was causing me to continue making poor financial decisions. This repeating pattern was holding me back from giving my business the funds it needed, AND also stopping my money spells from working.

You see, spells won't work long term if you keep making the same mistakes over and over and over.

I noticed this pattern resurface again recently when I was starting to spend money on advertising for my books. I was so afraid that I would spend more money than I made back and that I would end up destroying my business. I put off creating ads until a successful business mentor literally *gave* me money out of her pocket to use for my ads. (She were tired of watching me fret over a very normal business expense.)

I started my ads and, surprise, surprise, my earnings increased considerably. Then the next month, I made even more, and my income has grown ever since.

It was like the universe was just *waiting* for me to break my negative patterns so that it could send me the money I'd been trying to manifest for so long.

How To Shift The Energy

If you find you're getting stuck in an old energetic pattern, break the cycle. You can tell you're in a negative pattern if you keep getting close to manifesting your desire, but then somehow you always end up backsliding.

Maybe you always get bored with a romantic partner and dump them, only to regret it later. Maybe you give up learning a new skill because you notice everyone else is learning quicker than you. Maybe you overeat one day, and decide that this "eating healthy" thing is a lost cause.

Break the cycle by doing something different. I don't care if it turns out to be a good decision or a bad decision—just make sure it's a DIFFERENT decision. Then the universe, your higher power, your deities, or whatever you believe in will finally be able to send you your desire because you've opened up a new channel of energy.

Give it a try and see! If you feel like telling me about your energetic patterns and how you broke them, send me an email at julie@magicalpowerwithin.com. I'd love to hear about your breakthroughs!

You Didn't Wait Long Enough.

I tried starting many different businesses before I saw any kind financial return for my efforts. This was so frustrating because I would sometimes work for fourteen hours straight on my laptop. My family was so confused about what I was doing with my life, and my friends thought I was crazy for not getting a "real job".

It was especially painful for me to see other entrepreneurs making money a lot faster than me.

I had my witchcraft blog for two years before I started breaking even on my business costs. Then it took two more years after that to turn a profit.

You want to know what turned the tide?

One book.

One of my books took off—no idea why—and that started paying all the bills. Amazing, right?

My point is, don't give up on your spells.

You never know if everything will change tomorrow, and just because something is taking a long time, doesn't mean it's not on the way. It takes a long time to drive from Chicago to California. It takes a long time to grow your hair out after you get a pixie cut.

But remember what I said before—that the universe will meet you halfway. That's only going to happen if you STAY THE COURSE.

How To Shift The Energy

The lesson here is to keep the faith, my witchy friend. Keep the faith. I know what you really want is coming—but you've got to keep your energy joyful and expectant. It could happen tomorrow, next week, or next year.

I'd also recommend you learn about the backgrounds of the people who have achieved what you want. People love to talk about overnight success, but every entrepreneur who I've studied wasn't actually an overnight success. They had a whole bunch of businesses fail before finding one that worked for them.

Don't believe the hype. Sure, spells can and DO happen quickly, but many, many more spells manifest slowly and steadily.

You Didn't Actually Want It.

Let's talk about my failed love spell with my ex-boyfriend, Lou. You knew I'd have to bring that guy up again, didn't you?

I choose to believe that this universe is a generous and loving place. I believe that we are supposed to get the things we want, and that if we weren't supposed to have it, we wouldn't desire it.

I believe—beyond a shadow of a doubt—that I wanted Lou, specifically Lou, and no one else.

So if I wanted to be with Lou so bad, why didn't I get him?

The current reality is that Lou got married to someone else—after making me think that he was romantically interested in me.

I don't get to be with Lou. Period. How do I make sense of that as a powerful witch? Is this some cruel joke played on me by the universe?

As I've said before, I felt like magic had let me down big time. I'd seen so much success with magic, and to have this happen broke my heart.

Eventually, I made peace with this outcome, and I started to change my mind about Lou. Hindsight gave me some much needed perspective.

I now believe that when I had cast all those love spells to bring Lou and me together, my *energy* was actually asking for something completely different.

I had wanted Lou to be my romantic partner because I believed him and I were soulmates.

My desire for Lou was actually a disguise for an even deeper, more fulfilling desire—a desire to be loved by someone who understood me and loved me for me. I wanted a partner who would celebrate all my quirks, imperfections, mood swings, and my special brand of humor. I wanted someone who would see me at my worst and still love me.

I thought that person was Lou, but he wasn't.

Would I really want a man who lies about being engaged? Would I want a man who leads women on because it's an ego boost? Would I want a man who emotionally cheats with an ex-girlfriend?

No. That's not love.

That's why I believe the reason my love spell with Lou didn't work was because I didn't actually want him. I wanted a version of Lou that only existed in my head.

I'm still looking for my romantic partner, but I

believe he's out here. I also believe that the love spells I cast have been bringing my and my soul mate one step closer every single day.

✯

How To Shift The Energy

Hold some mental and emotional space for the idea that maybe, just maybe, the thing you wanted wasn't *really* what you wanted. Then keep your eyes open for the real deal.

It will show up, and when it does, you are going to appreciate the heck out if it.

FINAL THOUGHTS ON SPELLCASTING

My Favorite Spellcasting Hack
BE A MAGNET.

When I look back on any failed spell, I often see that I was forcing stuff to happen.

I always excused it because I'm a brilliant genius, and of course I know what's best for everyone. Who cares if I have to bend people and situations to my all-powerful will? It's for the greater good!

Just kidding. Sort of.

In order to counteract this Machiavellian tendency of mine, **I think about a magnet.**

Magnets are great at attracting things. That's literally their purpose for existing. If you have a strong magnet, things will fly through the air to latch onto it. Paperclips, kitchen knives, pins, earrings, and other magnets are naturally attracted just because of what the magnet is.

A magnet doesn't need to take any action. It is inherently attractive.

The spell you cast will (hopefully) magnetize you. It will put you into the same vibration as your desire, and because of the Law of Attraction, that desire will float through the universe, crossing black holes, deserts, and Atlanta traffic to get to you.

You don't have to blast yourself into the ether, grab that desire with your trembling fist, and squeeze it like an orange in a juicer until it manifests in your physical reality.

Forcing things won't attract your desire any faster. It might even repel your desire.

Think about when someone's trying to force you to do something you don't want to do.

Do you do it?

Maybe, but you'll probably feel resentment about it. You might still say no, and the other person's pushiness will make you dig in your heels even more.

Not think about what a magnet does if you flip it around and try to jam it up against another magnet. Maybe you can make them stay together for a short period of time—but only if you keep your hands on them and keep pushing them into each other.

The moment you let go, the pieces fly away from each other. Sure, we, witches, have the power to jam things together and hold them there... for a while.

You might have seen that happen with different things throughout your life.

I suspect this is partly what happened with Lou. I grabbed hold of him and dragged him into my energetic field. It kind of worked until he realized what was going on and pulled away. Then he resumed moving along his own path—the one he had been on before I'd commandeered his free will with my hurricane of magical love spells.

You can *try* to force things.

I've done it, and I know I'll probably continue to do it—old habits, and all that.

But when I force things, it's never had the lasting results I wanted.

It feels like a temporary high, but what comes up, must go down. That ride back down has been pretty painful for me.

Wouldn't you rather get yourself in alignment with your magical desires, and watch as that glittering bubble of your desire floats through the air and plops down into the palm of your hand?

Tips For Attracting Your Desire

Visualizations

- Think about the energy it takes to coax a cat out to play with you.
- Meditate on the image of a butterfly fluttering over and landing on your shoulder.

Magical Tools

- Hold a magnet in your hand as you visualize your intention.
- Place a magnet on your altar if you want some extra attracting energy.

Other Fun Stuff

- For a money spell, place some dollar bills in a money clip and stick it to your fridge with a magnet.
- For a love spell, write down everything you desire in a romantic relationship. Then fold up the paper and place it between two magnets. Set the paper and magnets on your altar or somewhere you'll see them. One magnet will represent you. The other will represent your ideal partner. Together, you two will attract each other no matter where you both are or what you're doing.

Why Witchcraft Is Like Driving A Car

If you've gone through this entire book and you don't think any of these reasons had anything to do with why your spell didn't work, don't panic.

Sit down.

Take a deep breath.

Drink a cup of water or something.

And know that it's OK, and NORMAL to have no idea why something didn't work out. Sometimes the answer will come to you in the future—in the lyrics of a song on your music app, in the feeling of peace you get after you throw up your arms and say, "My spell didn't work. Whatever. No big deal", or in the conversation you strike up with a stranger on the street.

We don't always get to see the full picture from where we are as humans living on planet earth and accepting that is a big step in freeing up a lot of your energy.

Witchcraft helped me physically, mentally, and emotionally gain some control over my life, but I know that magic will only take me as far as I allow myself to go.

If I'm too afraid to take a risk that feels brave, expansive and exhilarating, witchcraft won't take away my fear or uncertainty. Witchcraft can't change who you are. *You* have to do that. You have to make a commitment to yourself to go after what you want, believe in yourself, and above all, to love yourself fiercely, madly, and deeply.

No one will love you like you.

Think of witchcraft like a car. Cars can do all kinds of amazing things like get us places faster than our legs, play fun music, let us feel the wind in our hair, and light the road ahead for us.

However, if you don't get into that car and turn on the ignition, you're not going anywhere. You have to start the engine, choose your destination, and steer the car all the way there. You have to make decisions to drive slower or faster, to pass people or pull over at a rest stop.

Witchcraft is like your car. It will work if you do your part.

And, like spells, if that car isn't working properly, there's usually a reason. The brakes need to be replaced. You ran out of gas. The tire's got a leak. Sometimes, a mechanic can't pinpoint the problem or it's a combination of things. In that case, you might decide that it's not worth fixing the car, and you'd be much happier getting a new car. This is how I feel about my spell with Lou not happening. I'm not going to keep pouring energy into manifesting that relationship when I'd much rather cast a new love spell.

So go forth, my witchy friend! Cast your spells and believe in your own power. You're the one in control.

A Note From The Author

Hi there, Witch!

Thanks for picking up this book! I hope it helped you on your magical journey.

If you want to learn more ways to practice simple, secular witchcraft, be sure to pick up a copy of this book of spells, and my free Beginner Witch Starter kit with printables, correspondences, meditations, and magical journaling prompts. Use the link below to get both of those!

https://whitewitchacademy.com/freebies

Also, be sure to check out the other witchy books in the **White Witch Academy Textbook series.** You can find them here:

https://whitewitchacademy.com/books

If you're on social media,
follow me on Instagram or Tik Tok
@whitewitchacademy
Or send me an email at
julie@magicalpowerwithin.com

Lastly, **if you enjoyed this book leave a review so other witches can decide if this book is for them!** Reviews help me out so much and I appreciate the feedback.

Thank you for reading. I hope this book bought a little joy and magic to your life!

Until next time,

Julie Wilder

Also by Julie Wilder

What Type of Witch Are You?
How to Become A Witch
Why Didn't My Spell Work?
Beginner Witch's Guide to Grimoires
Tarot for Beginner Witches

Printed in Great Britain
by Amazon